Xtreme Athletes

Tito Ortiz

Xtreme Athletes

Tito Ortiz

Jeff Savage

MORGAN REYNOLDS
PUBLISHING

Greensboro, North Carolina

Xtreme Athletes

Brock Lesnar
Apolo Ohno
Tito Ortiz
Danica Patrick
Michael Phelps
Kelly Slater
Michelle Wie
Shaun White

Xtreme Athletes: Tito Ortiz

Library of Congress Cataloging-in-Publication Data

Savage, Jeff, 1961-.
 Tito Ortiz / by Jeff Savage.
   p. cm. -- (Xtreme athletes)
 Includes bibliographical references and index.
 ISBN 978-1-59935-184-1 -- ISBN 978-1-59935-210-7
(e-book) 1. Ortiz,
Tito, 1975- 2. Martial artists--United States--Biography. 3. Mixed
martial
arts--Biography. I. Title.
 GV1113.O77S29 2012
 796.8092--dc23
 [B]
                                                    2011019145

Printed in the United States of America
First Edition

For Laurie and Mike Jones—the undisputed
Ultimate Fighting Champions in my book

Tito Ortiz during his UFC
light heavyweight match
in Las Vegas in 2008

Contents

Jacob "Tito" Ortiz is a Mexican American star of mixed martial arts, or the sport more popularly known as Ultimate Fighting.

one
A Rough Start

Bang! Tito Ortiz is rocked on the chin. Japan's Yuki Kondo sends a wicked flying knee kick that knocks Tito off his feet. The crowd at Ariake Arena in Tokyo, Japan, roars at the sight of the young mixed martial arts champion on his back.

Kondo's vicious kick would have knocked out most fighters. Not Tito. He is nearly indestructible. It doesn't seem to matter that six months earlier he had been run over by a bus.

Tito jumps to his feet, grabs Kondo, and yells, "Is that all you've got!" He slams Kondo to the ground, squeezes him with his thighs, and pounds him with punches and elbows. When Kondo tries to escape Tito grabs him in a cobra choke. Kondo can't breathe and has no choice but to quit. He taps out.

Tito's victory over Kondo took place at the 2000 Ultimate Fighting Championship (UFC). It marked

the arrival of a reign of fury that would grip the Mixed Martial Arts (MMA) world. Such brutality was nothing new to Tito. His life had been a stormy battle for survival from the very beginning.

Jacob Christopher Ortiz was born in Southern California on January 23, 1975. His mother, Joyce, had three sons from a previous marriage. His father, Samuel, met Joyce a year before Tito was born. Joyce and Samuel were never officially married. Samuel served several months in prison as a convicted drug dealer. Samuel nicknamed his son "Tito." The name Tito translates to "tyrant" in Spanish. In Tito's case, the meaning was befitting.

Tito lived together with his parents and three half brothers—Jim, Mike, and Marty. Tito was the youngest by five years, and his older brothers constantly picked on him. They played cruel pranks, like tying him to the chimney on the roof. Eventually, the bullying would make Tito tough. But at the time Tito cried often. There were occasions when the four boys got along. They lived in Huntington Beach within walking distance of the Pacific Ocean, and sometimes the brothers walked through alleys to the beach where they splashed in the waves or played catch with a football. Sometimes they used the football as a way to steal. They would

Huntington Beach, California

throw the football to the towels of others while those people were in the water. They would run to the football, drop to the sand, and rummage through their belongings to find money. "I was too young to know that what I was doing was a crime," Tito says now. "It just seemed like another fun thing to do."

Tito's favorite childhood passion was fishing. He liked to cast a line from the ocean pier. When the family went camping, he fished at Lake Elsinore or in the streams at Caspers Wilderness Park. His father

taught him how to clean the fish. Samuel also showed his son how to shoot a gun, and they went hunting a few times. Tito hadn't started kindergarten yet when he fired a twelve-gauge shotgun for the first time. The force of the gun's recoil flattened him and left him crying on his back.

Tito had long hair that went down his back. On his first day of school at Eader Elementary, he was teased by other kids and told that he looked like a girl. Tito cried at home to his mother. She cut his hair into a Mohawk. Such a style was unacceptable at school. So his mother shaved off his hair. Now Tito was teased for being bald. Tito was big for his age, and his size prevented some kids from making it worse for him. But Tito's early experience at school was nothing compared to the misery at home.

Tito's parents were drug addicts. They smoked marijuana every day. Samuel worked in construction, and he was able to go to work in the morning, but not before he got high. Joyce kept her boys fed and wearing clean clothes, but she usually smoked a joint as she cooked and cleaned. Tito's parents were stoned so often that they hardly noticed what their sons were doing. Tito's three brothers smoked pot too. They taught Tito how to do it. Tito smoked marijuana for the first time when he was five years old. He remembers getting dizzy and falling. Afterward he got a terrible headache. But he did it again. Then he started drinking beer.

Things were about to get worse. Tito's father underwent back surgery. At home afterward, the medicine prescribed by the doctor was not relieving his pain. Samuel's brother, Reuben, gave him another drug to take. It was heroin. This powerful drug worked—temporarily. When it wore off, Tito's father wanted more. He gave some to Tito's mother. Soon they were hooked. Heroin is expensive. Tito watched as his parents began selling items from the house to pay for the drug. The family continued to go on regular outings like camping or fishing on a friend's boat, but now they would sneak off with their needle to inject themselves with heroin. At home, they ran out of things to sell. So they reverted to stealing. Tito's father stole things from work. Tito's mother stole items from department stores and then returned the items to get a refund in cash. They used the money to buy more heroin. Sometimes they bought food, but other times, they went through their neighbors' garbage cans to find something to eat.

Tito was six years old when his three brothers were sent away. Tito's mother and father could no longer afford to care for them. They asked a family friend to raise the boys. And just like that they were gone. Tito saw the boys on holidays and other occasions. He wondered if his parents would send him away too.

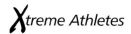

It wasn't long before Tito's father got so sick from using heroin that he began staying in bed for days at a time. He lost his regular job. He took odd jobs when he was able. The family could not afford to pay the rent and were forced to leave their house. They moved to the other side of Interstate 405 into a rough neighborhood in nearby Santa Ana. They lived in that house for just a few months until they were evicted again. A few months later, they moved again. And then they moved again.

By the time Tito reached second grade, he had already been to four elementary schools. He never told his teachers or classmates what life was like for him at home. He pretended life was as normal as he

Santa Ana, California

imagined it was for everyone else at school. He struggled with academics, especially reading and writing. He did a little better at math and science. Some days he skipped school entirely. He would walk to school, then sneak down a different street to a bus stop, where the municipal bus would take him to Newport Beach. He would spend the day fishing from the pier.

Being at home was worse for Tito than going to school. He hated watching his parents shooting heroin. They cooked the drug before injecting it into their veins. Sometimes they did it behind a door or a curtain so he couldn't see, but he always knew. The smell of burned matches gave it away. Tito hated being in the house so much that he would leave. He would

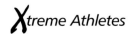

be gone for hours at a time, sometimes all night. He would hang out with friends at their houses. When it was time for them to get ready for bed, he would leave and walk around the neighborhood streets in the dark. His parents didn't seem to notice or care.

Tito stole clothes from department stores. He stole food from grocery stores. He had learned to steal from his parents. He figured it was the one thing he was good at doing. One time Tito and a friend sneaked into someone's backyard to steal marijuana plants. They sawed off two large plants and took off. Tito scampered down the sidewalk toward home when he saw his father approaching and yelling at him. Tito did not know what to do. He stopped directly in front of his father, held out a plant and said, "Dad, look what I got for you." His father smiled. Tito had escaped his father's wrath.

Tito and his parents were forced to leave their house again, and this time, they had no money to rent another place. So they survived any way they could. Sometimes they lived in other people's garages. Sometimes they lived in their car. Once in a while, when they had enough money left over from buying drugs and food, they stayed for a few nights at a cheap motel. Those nights were special to Tito because he would get a warm shower. For a while, they lived in a small trailer next to a campground. Tito's parents continued to take illegal drugs. One time, Tito remembers warning his parents that the police were coming, and together they ran from the trailer and jumped over a fence to hide. Tito never told his friends at school where he lived. Sometimes he was invited to their house to play. He certainly never invited them to his place because he was too embarrassed to be known as a homeless boy.

Tito's escape was fishing. He struggled with reading, but not when he read about fishing. His father had taken him out on the ocean on a fishing boat a few times, and as the fishermen reeled in their catch, Tito could identify the type of fish. The boat's owner, Mark Thompson, was impressed with Tito's fishing knowledge, and he offered Tito a job cleaning the boat in exchange for free fishing. Tito jumped at the opportunity. Tito worked and fished on the boat until evening. He loved those hours away from his parents and their drugs. He even got two new fishing poles, and he took the fishing poles home with him. The next day, the fishing poles were gone. His father had sold them for drug money.

On the afternoons that Tito wasn't on the boat, he was getting into trouble with his mischievous friends. He was ten years old when he joined a gang. F Troop was one of the toughest gangs in Santa Ana. The leaders were sixteen-year-olds, and most of the members were at least fourteen. Tito was big for his age, and he was certainly streetwise. He had been hanging out

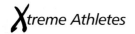

with members of F Troop for a few months when he was invited to officially join the gang. In order to be accepted, he had to get jumped in. Tito was forced to go through a line of about eight members who beat on him. As they kicked and punched him, Tito fought back as best as he could. When it was over, his face was bloody and swollen, but he had stayed conscious. He was in the gang. For Tito, being a member of F Troop felt special, like he was in a family.

Tito did a lot of harm to himself and others as a member of F Troop. He smoked marijuana and drank beer. He sniffed paint and glue to get high. To get money for the drugs, he broke into cars and stole stereos. Tito was living just like his parents. Part of F Troop's turf was Centennial Regional Park, and they beat members of rival gangs who dared set foot in the park. Tito enjoyed participating in the brawls. But as much as he felt a sense of belonging, he knew that gang life wasn't right. "I knew the stuff I was doing wasn't good," Tito said. "Something in my heart was telling me that I wasn't being a good person."

At home, Tito's parents finally sought help from a doctor to try to break their heroin addiction. Tito's mother was able to do it; Tito's father was not. Samuel left the family and moved in with his mother. Tito and his mother were alone now. Life was calmer.

against a van with other gang members when a strange car pulled up. Someone from the car called out. Someone from F Troop answered back. Bang! A shot was fired. The boy standing next to Tito dropped dead. All at once, guns came out and bullets were flying. Tito jumped over a concrete wall. He ran home as fast as he could. He told his mother what happened. "That's it!" she said. "We're getting out of Santa Ana. Pack your bags. We're leaving." Tito's mother said they would move back to Huntington Beach and rent a place. Tito didn't argue. He was already afraid of guns and he had just seen another boy get killed. He wanted out of the gang. But to be allowed to leave F Troop, Tito knew he had to be jumped out. He gritted his teeth and suffered the same beating as when he joined the gang. He was out.

Tito makes an appearance at the Ultimate Fighting Championship at Mandalay Bay in June 2004

two

Getting a Grip

Tito was a record-setter at Dwyer Middle School—but not in a good way. By his count, he spent sixty-four days in detention, the most of any seventh-grader in school history. Like many thirteen-year-olds, Tito didn't like waking up early in the morning to go to school. Unlike most, his mother didn't make him. So Tito was often tardy. Then there were the fights. You might think that attending a school just six blocks from the beach would have a calming effect on a boy. Not so for Tito. He was edgy. He looked for trouble—and he found it. Fights sometimes included a chain, a skateboard, a car hood ornament, anything he or his combatant could get their hands on. Most times, it was just fists. In either case, Tito won his share of fights, and he lost some too.

Tito's mother met a man named Michael Johnson, and before long they were married. Now Tito had a

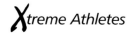

stepfather in the house. Tito's older half-brother Marty moved in with them. Meanwhile, Jim was living with a girlfriend, and Mike was in juvenile hall for assault. Tito's stepfather provided some financial stability for the family. But Tito was unhappy. He continued to smoke marijuana, drink alcohol, and sniff glue. His mother knew about his drug use and told him to stop. Tito didn't listen. Then things got worse. Tito started smoking crack cocaine. It is an insidious drug that fries your brain. Tito didn't care. He wasn't thinking straight. His friends Nathan, Ricky, and Nacho did it—so why shouldn't he?

There is no telling the damage this drug did to Tito, but there is no doubt it provoked him into making poor choices. He stole things from stores and parked cars. He even broke into a post office to steal an American flag. But he really lost his head the night he committed a robbery by sudden snatching, otherwise known as strong-arm robbery. If convicted of such a crime, the offender could be sentenced to prison. That night, Tito and some friends stood outside a nightclub called Taxi's, waiting for a victim. When a man came out the door, Tito and his friends jumped him. They started beating the man and grabbing for his wallet. Somehow the man escaped and ran back into the nightclub. Moments later, the man reappeared with others. Tito and his friends ran. The men chased them. Tito sensed that the men would catch him, so he did the only thing he could think of. He slowed down to let them catch up. He pretended he was with them. "Let's get those guys!" Tito shouted as he ran with the men. The trick worked. Tito waited for his chance to break from the group, and then he sneaked home.

As a freshman at Huntington Beach High School, Tito continued on his destructive path. If things didn't change, he probably would end up like his parents once were—hooked on heroin and homeless or dead. Luckily for Tito, everything changed.

Tito's mother prompted the change. One afternoon she caught Tito doing drugs with Ricky and Nacho in the backyard. She sent Ricky and Nacho home. Then she laid into Tito. She told him how those boys were nothing but trouble—and that he was allowing them to destroy his life. She told him how he needed to take control, that to have a better chance for a good life, he needed to find another type of friend. Tito cried. But this time he listened.

The next day, Tito came home with Eric Escobedo. Eric was on the high school wrestling team. Tito loved watching professional wrestling on television. He enjoyed the smack talk and the crazy hype. He didn't realize pro wrestling was fake. Tito asked Eric to show him some wrestling moves. Eric grabbed Tito and tossed him to the floor. He locked him up, flipped him on his back, and spun him around. He controlled

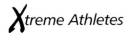

Tito with ease, as though he were moving a checker to another square. Tito was a strong young man. How could someone the same size handle him like that? Tito was fascinated. He asked Eric to take him to a wrestling practice.

The next day, Tito met Bob Rice, the school's wrestling coach. Tito looked around the gym. "Where's the ring?" he asked. The coach explained that real

Two high school students wrestling in an official school match

wrestling took place on a mat, not in a ring with ropes, and that Tito was confusing it with fake wrestling. Tito had a hard time believing that pro wrestling was fake. He asked Coach Rice if he could join the team. The coach told Tito to demonstrate his ability by grappling with a varsity wrestler. Tito was helpless against the experienced wrestler—until the moment when he grabbed him by the hair and started pulling

his head back. Coach Rice jumped in to stop it. Tito thought it was a wrestling move. After all, it was what he had seen on TV. Tito had a lot to learn about real wrestling. Coach Rice sensed that Tito was eager to learn, so he agreed to allow him to join the team.

Tito's first competitive match ended in a blink. He wrestled Michael Biss from Westchester High School. In the first round, Biss shot in, took Tito down, put him in a cradle hold, and pinned him. Tito got to his feet and staggered back to his team at the side of the mat. He cried and asked Coach Rice what happened. The coach calmly described the moves Biss used to subdue him. Tito was angry that he could be controlled like that. More important, he was anxious to learn how to counter it. At practice the next day, he was taught how to make and escape a cradle. Each day he learned more moves at practice. For Tito, regular practice time wasn't enough. He came to practice early. He stayed late. He practiced at Eric's house over the weekend. The practice paid off. In his second match, he pinned his opponent with a head and arm lock. Tito's desire to learn was obvious to Coach Rice, who immediately put him on the varsity team. Tito was thrilled.

Suddenly grades mattered to Tito. To compete in sports at school, athletes are required to maintain a certain grade-point average. If Tito wanted to wrestle for Huntington Beach High, he needed to improve his grades. This meant he had to get up early and arrive at school on time, pay attention in class, and do his homework. Tito was never allergic to school; he just didn't see a reason to try—until now. As a sophomore he wrestled in the 152-pound weight class and registered a solid 25-15 record. More impressive to those who knew Tito was his academic success. He recorded a 3.46 grade-point average. Wrestling had turned him around.

Unfortunately for Tito, school wrestling is not a year-round sport. If it were, he likely would have dodged trouble for good. As it was, when the wrestling season ended, so did Tito's focus on good behavior and academics. He lapsed into his familiar bad habits—and this time it got worse. Tito continued to steal from cars. One day at the start of summer vacation, he actually stole the car itself. At least, that's the way the judge saw it. Tito was scrounging through the car when he found the ignition key. He decided to take the car for a joy ride. It was stick shift, and Tito was unfamiliar with how to drive it. He somehow managed to grind and muscle the car to his friend Eric's house. But as he pulled into Eric's driveway, he lost control, and the car bashed into the Escobedo's parked car. Eric's parents were furious. Instead of calling Tito's mother, they called the police. Tito was arrested and charged with grand theft auto. In court, the judge sentenced Tito to serve thirty-nine days in juvenile hall—a prison for minors.

Tito certainly didn't want to be locked up, but he had expected it to happen some day. His father spent time in prison, and his half brother did time in juvenile hall. To Tito, serving time was not outlandish. He found it to be somewhat like detention—except that the days seemed to drag on forever. He lived in a small cell with just a bed, toilet, and sink. Such meager accommodations were nothing knew to Tito, of course. He had lived in a garage, a car, and a tiny trailer. Food was served to him through a slot in the cell door. He was released from his cell each day for five hours of classes and a shower. He avoided trouble by keeping to himself. At night he did push-ups and sit ups to build strength. He thought often about wrestling.

Back at school for his junior year, Tito found out the wrestling team had a new coach. Paul Herrera took over, and Tito connected with Coach Herrera instantly. At home, Tito shared some close moments with his stepfather, Mike Johnson, like the time Mike sewed Tito's first wrestling letter into his jacket. But Tito felt that Mike was in the house to be with Tito's mother and that he was just in the way. He also saw his real father from time to time, but Tito did not trust Samuel Ortiz. Tito remembers getting a moped for his sixteenth birthday. His father asked to borrow it and rode away. He didn't come back. Tito learned later that his father sold the moped for drug money.

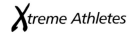

Tito did not have a true father figure, but he looked to Coach Herrera for guidance. Herrera made sure Tito got to school on time and kept up with his studies. Tito was one of the top wrestlers on the team that year, and he led the Oilers to the league title. But as soon as the wrestling season ended, Tito was back in trouble again. He was standing in the school hallway with a girl one day when a group of boys walked by. One of them called the girl a degrading name. Tito stopped the boy and asked if there was a misunderstanding. The boy repeated what he said and asked Tito what he was going to do about it. Tito was enraged. The boy's friends stood with him, so Tito knew he was outnumbered.

The next morning, Tito spotted the boy alone in the cafeteria and walked up and punched him. The blow broke the boy's shoulder. Tito went to class. An hour later, the on-campus policeman approached Tito at his desk and told him he was under arrest for assault. He was handcuffed in the classroom and taken to jail.

Tito was found guilty and sentenced to twenty-three days in juvenile hall. This stint was similar to his first one, except that he earned his way into the weight room by volunteering to run in a 5K race. By now, Tito was fully devoted to strength training—and anything else it took to improve at wrestling.

When he got out Coach Herrera wanted Tito to wrestle his senior year at 160 pounds. Tito weighed 174.

He had nine days to cut fourteen pounds before the official California Interscholastic Federation (CIF) weigh-in. He ate carefully and logged countless hours of cardio training. He pedaled a stationary bike, jogged through the neighborhood, and did thousands of jumping jacks. At the weigh-in, the scale read 160.8. Tito excused himself and went to the boys' locker room to vomit. He reweighed in at 160 pounds exactly. Tito's senior season was stellar. He amassed a record of 56-3. Thirty-six of his wins were pins. He was the best wrestler on his team, first in his league, and tops in the county. Even better than all of that, wrestling probably saved Tito from a long term in prison.

Tito was still hanging out with Ricky and Nacho. The other boys were mixed up with a ruthless gang now. Tito wanted no part of that, but he still felt an allegiance to his boyhood friends. One night Nacho tried to convince Tito to join him in some gang business. Nacho said he needed to make a delivery. Tito declined the offer. Nacho said it wouldn't take long and that he could use the help. Tito wouldn't give in. He said wrestling came first, and he had practice the next day. Nacho was arrested later that night for possession of drugs, assault rifles, and bulletproof vests. He was sentenced to prison for twenty-five years to life.

Tito during a news conference in Las Vegas in 2006.

three
Seizing Opportunity

Tito was one of the top wrestlers in the state. His will to succeed was fierce. He also flourished in the classroom—but only during wrestling season. If only he had dedicated himself to school more consistently. Major colleges wanted to give Tito an athletic scholarship because they wanted him to wrestle for their program—he was that good. Tito could have gone to an excellent university essentially for free, but his grades weren't good enough and he did not qualify academically.

When Tito graduated from high school on June 14, 1993, it was quite an accomplishment, considering everything he had overcome, but it could have been much more. As it was, Tito had no direction at this point. All he knew is that he had to leave the house. Mike Johnson kicked Tito out.

Johnson figured that if Tito wasn't doing something productive, like attending college, then it was time for him to go out and make it on his own. Tito's mother cried and gave her son $800.

Ortiz moved in with his brother Marty and his girlfriend and used the money his mother gave him to buy a car. He got a job with a moving company hauling people's furniture. It was grueling work, but it kept him in shape. He also worked some nights as a bouncer at a nightclub. His job at the club was to ensure that customers stayed in line and obeyed the rules. Once in a while he had to get physical with a patron. This is where his wrestling experience came in handy. He put one unruly man in a headlock, lifted him in the air, and threw him out the door. He was getting paid to be a tough guy—and he liked it.

Ortiz wondered about his future. For the most part, he was lost. The only real positive he had in his life was his girlfriend Kristin. They knew each other from high school, and after graduation they began hanging out as friends. One night, while out at a movie, an unfamiliar feeling overwhelmed Ortiz. He realized he was falling in love. Kristin felt the same way. They were together every day after that.

A few months went by, and Kristin's birthday arrived. Ortiz wanted to get his girlfriend something special. But he didn't have much money. He borrowed Kristin's car and returned later with a giant bubble gum machine. Kristin's mother got a phone call the

Silhouette of dancers at a nightclub

next day from the Huntington Beach police. A note-
book with Kristin's name on it had fallen out of her
car at the restaurant where Ortiz stole the bubble gum
machine. Kristin's mother made Ortiz return the sto-
len property and turn himself in to the police. He was
sent to jail for two weeks.

By chance, Ortiz bumped into his wrestling coach
Paul Herrera one day. Coach Herrera was friends with

An aerial view of Huntington Beach, California

the wrestling coach at Golden West College—the local community college in Huntington Beach. He told Ortiz he could probably wrestle for the school, and get his tuition and books paid for because of it. Ortiz went home and thought about it. He hadn't wrestled in nearly two years. But it was a skill he had worked hard to master, and if he didn't seize this opportunity, he probably would never get another chance.

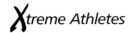

He certainly knew he didn't want to haul furniture for the rest of his life.

Ortiz went with Herrera to the college the next day where they met with Coach Raoul Duarte. Ortiz convinced Coach Duarte to give him a chance. He was awarded financial aid and added to the wrestling team. He happily quit his job with the moving company and enrolled in classes. Kristin took classes with him.

Ortiz studied special education. He would have liked to someday be a teacher and a high school wrestling coach. He took his studies seriously because he knew he wanted to make something of himself, and deep down, he didn't think there was much of a future in wrestling.

In the meantime, on the wrestling mat, he destroyed his junior college competition. The techniques he had learned in high school, combined with his brute strength, were too much for his opponents. In fact, he never lost a match. He won the state title. He also got noticed in another way. He kept his hair cropped short and dyed it a different color for each tournament. Students at Golden West College came to the meets just to see Ortiz's hair. The attention was something new for Ortiz and he soaked it up.

After the season, Ortiz got more help from Paul Herrera. Ortiz was told that a local mixed martial arts fighter named Tank Abbott was searching for a wrestling partner. Ortiz knew plenty about this new extreme sport that combined wrestling, boxing, martial arts, and street fighting. He was captivated by the ruthless battles and crazy antics of the fighters in the Ultimate Fighting Championship (UFC). He was especially intrigued to see someone like Jerry Bohlander, a wrestler he had defeated in high school, competing in the sport. If Bohlander could do it, Ortiz thought, how hard could it be? Ortiz decided he would give mixed martial arts a try.

Ortiz preferred to limit his training with Abbott to wrestling at first, and he told Abbott so. Abbott was pleased to hear it since that was the weakest part of his game. As Ortiz soon discovered, he could control Abbott on the ground with relative ease. Abbott was loud and obnoxious, and Ortiz sensed that Abbott resented him for being superior at wrestling. Still, they trained together through the summer. While Abbott learned a few wrestling moves, Ortiz got his first glimpse into what it took to be an ultimate fighter. He saw that it required an array of skills such as stand-up punches, leg kicks, defense, grappling, stamina, and ground-and-pound techniques.

Abbott impressed upon Ortiz the importance of image. Ortiz learned that if you simply showed up for battle and then quietly left, you would hardly be noticed. But if you boasted in the days leading up to your fight, and if you made outlandish statements afterward, win or lose, people would remember you.

And they would want to see you fight again. Sure, if you lost enough times, you would eventually be dismissed as a pushover. Conversely, if you won repeatedly, your seeming invincibility would overcome a bland personality. But if you were like most fighters who sported a mix of wins and losses, your behavior would determine your popularity. The more popular you were, the more likely matchmakers would want to sign you to another fight—and the more money you would make.

Back at Golden West College, Ortiz won the 1997 state wrestling title with a perfect 28-0 record. Soon after, he got a phone call from Tank Abbott. Ortiz was being invited to compete in a mixed martial arts event. Since the UFC was still in its infancy, fighters didn't make much money. This didn't matter to Ortiz at the time. In order to wrestle in college and receive financial aid he needed to be an amateur. If he got paid in any sport, even once, he would be considered a professional and thereby lose his amateur status. So Ortiz was not interested in the money—yet. He agreed to fight because he saw it as a challenge. He trained with Abbott and learned the basics of Brazilian Jiu-Jitsu, a martial art that features ground fighting moves like chokeholds and armlocks.

Ortiz made his Ultimate Fighting Championship debut on May 30, 1997. It was billed as UFC 13: The Ultimate Force. The event drew thousands of fans to an arena in Augusta, Georgia. Many more purchased the fight on television via pay-per-view. The event was structured in a tournament format where the winners of the first-round fights advanced to the final round. However, Ortiz's lightweight match was an alternate bout, meaning he would fight just once, unless something happened to one of the first-round winners.

Ortiz was listed as a street fighter affiliated with Team Tank. His opponent was Wes Albritton, a fifth-degree black belt in karate. Ortiz stepped into the Octagon and paced back and forth. He saw the TV cameras aimed at him and heard the clamor of the crowd, and he was overcome by the magnitude of it. "I'm here!" he told himself. "Don't make a mistake."

The bell rang to start the fight, and Ortiz shot forward. He grabbed Albritton in a clinch by putting his arms under Albritton's and pulling up—a basic wrestling move called double underhooks. Ortiz threw Albritton to the ground and mounted him in an open guard by straddling his thighs over Albritton's chest. He began bashing Albritton's face with his fists and elbows. Within moments, Referee Joe Hamilton reached in to stop it. Ortiz jumped to his feet and was greeted by members of Team Tank. The fight lasted thirty-one seconds. The official result was victory by technical knockout, or TKO. One publication described it as a "short, brutal fight as Ortiz was easily a class above."

Ortiz celebrated in his dressing room. "I was pumped," he recalled. "Since it was on television, all my friends got to see me beating somebody up and I wasn't getting in trouble for doing it."

"The Octagon" is the official name of the eight-sided enclosure where UFC bouts are staged. The walls of the Octagon are made of metal fencing coated in vinyl. Foam padding covers the tops of the fence, and there's padding between each of the eight sections.

Later that night, the lightweight final appeared set. But one of the first-round winners, Enson Inoue, backed out because of vision problems. Ortiz was picked as the replacement. "I got thrown in against

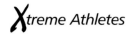

Guy Mezger," said Ortiz. "I didn't know who Guy Mezger." Mezger was the three-time state wrestling champion and accomplished mixed martial artist affiliated with the Lion's Den—the most dominant fight camp in the UFC at the time.

Ortiz decided he would attack Mezger as he did Albritton—and the strategy worked. He grabbed Mezger in a headlock and pounded him with knee kicks. He hooked Mezger's leg with a cradle and bombed him with punches and more knees. Mezger's face was gushing blood now, as he tried to block the blows with his hand. Just then, he appeared to tap out—signaling that he wanted to quit the fight. That is what it seemed to Ortiz and many in the crowd, anyway. Referee John McCarthy jumped in to stop the fight.

Ortiz won. Or did he? The referee told Ortiz he was stopping the fight so the ring doctor could check Mezger's cuts. Ortiz was confused. Did the rules permit that? Didn't Mezger tap? The referee told Ortiz that he did not see Mezger tap. McCarthy ruled the fight to continue and ordered a restart.

Ortiz shot in again, but this time Mezger sprawled and grabbed Ortiz around the neck in a guillotine choke. Ortiz couldn't breathe. He did not know how to escape this choke. He tapped out.

Ortiz took out his mouthpiece and threw it to the floor. He shook his head and swore. He thought the referee had robbed him by allowing the fight to continue earlier. Most observers agreed. "Ortiz got a raw deal," said UFC matchmaker Joe Silva. "He had Mezger in a lot of trouble, and Guy Mezger was not going to be able to get out of that position. If it had to be stopped because he's bleeding, well, then it's over. And they stopped and then re-started it. I felt bad for Tito."

Ortiz was angry, but in the dressing room, his spirits were lifted somewhat by the praise heaped on him. After all, he had dominated two fighters. The night had been a whirlwind of emotions, and Ortiz still had much to sort out, but he knew one thing—he was gripped by the thrill of UFC fighting.

A mixed martial arts competition

Tito poses for photographers at the
MGM Grand Hotel in Las Vegas in 2006.

four

The Huntington Beach Bad Boy

Ortiz was torn now. He loved everything about mixed martial arts. At a nightclub back home with Kristin, strangers treated him like he was a celebrity.

On the other hand, Ortiz was carving a path in wrestling. He was such a success his two years at Golden West that major college programs clamored for him. He had accepted an athletic scholarship from Cal State Bakersfield University and was scheduled to start school in three months. Ultimate fighting or wrestling—Ortiz had to choose.

Ortiz picked wrestling. He made a commitment to the school and felt he should see it through. He also still had visions of being a teacher, and getting a free education was an opportunity he couldn't pass up. He loaded a U-Haul truck with his belongings and made the three-hour drive north to Bakersfield, where he moved into a dormitory on campus.

Ortiz and his college wrestling coach did not get along. It wasn't the coach's stern demeanor that

A wrestler from Cal State Bakersfield (top) and his opponent from Iowa State compete in the heavyweight division of the NCAA Division 1 Wrestling Championships. These athletes are wrestling in the collegiate style (also known as folk style or scholastic style), a form of wrestling used in high school and university competitions.

Ortiz minded. It was what Ortiz perceived to be his disrespect toward the wrestlers. Ortiz tried to make the most of it. He especially enjoyed training with future National Collegiate Athletic Association (NCAA) champion Stephen Neal.

One day during the season, a man named Sal Garcia approached Ortiz. Garcia said he was connected to the UFC and that he wanted to be Ortiz's manager. "I have a plan that can make you a star," Garcia said. Ortiz appreciated Garcia's interest, but he declined. He said he would keep the offer in mind but that he wanted to stick with wrestling for now.

Garcia had a mixed martial arts gym in Bakersfield. Ortiz went there from time to time to watch the fighters, but he devoted his energy toward wrestling and it was paying off. Ortiz rolled through opponents and was likely headed for the college national championship tournament when a leg injury set him back. Ortiz wasn't sure what happened exactly, but doctors told him his leg was damaged due to a lack of blood circulation, and only antibiotics and a month of rest could repair it.

Ortiz stayed off his feet for four weeks. The coach never called to check on Ortiz. The wrestling season ended. Ortiz was so upset that he quit the team, quit school, and moved back to Huntington Beach, where he rented an apartment with Kristin. He figured it was time for one more change.

Ortiz called Sal Garcia. "I'd like to fight again. Would you like to manage me?" Ortiz asked.

"Sure. Yes, that's what I've been waiting for," Garcia replied.

Ortiz started an intense mixed martial arts training program at the Los Angeles Boxing Club. He learned Muay Thai from black belt trainer John Spencer Ellis. Muay Thai is a stand-up striking style using fists, elbows, knees, and feet. Ortiz considered Ellis the best Muay Thai kickboxing trainer in the world. He also used the success of UFC heavyweight champion Sebastiaan "Bas" Rutten for motivation. "Bas was my idol," Ortiz said. "People were just so scared of fighting him, he was, like, the man. I thought that was what I needed to do. If I train as hard as he does then one day I'll be as good as him."

Ortiz was primed to fight but repeated requests to the UFC from his manager Garcia went nowhere. Ortiz learned that Garcia wasn't as "connected" to the organization as he was led to believe. Garcia did come up with an idea to get Ortiz noticed. "We needed to create a persona," said the manager, "like Stone Cold Steve Austin from the WWF."

Garcia made a Tito Ortiz trading card. He took a picture of Ortiz in his backyard and hired a graphic designer to combine the photograph with statistics and information about Ortiz. The back of the trading card said this:

TITO ORTIZ
D.O.B. 1/23/75
WEIGHT 200
HEIGHT 6'2"
RECORD 9-1-0
HOME Huntington Beach, Ca.
Tito Ortiz returned to the U.F.C. . . . to become one of the most successful fighters in the history of mixed martial arts. Since returning, Tito has completely dominated the middle-weight division.

The information wasn't accurate, but the card would catch people's attention. Now Garcia needed to "sell" Ortiz to the UFC promoters. So he and Ortiz went to the next UFC event—in Brazil.

In the days leading up to the event, they passed out trading cards to everyone associated with the organization. They met UFC owner Bob Meyrowitz and matchmakers Joe Silva and John Peretti. Silva remembers his meeting with Ortiz in Brazil. "He's a hard person to miss," Silva said. "He just has that look. He's like a walking caricature. And he had T-shirts. And he had cards. And I was like, 'Who is this guy?' And I'd remembered him from fighting UFC, but he had only made that brief appearance, and then you

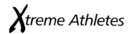

hadn't seen him for a while. He was pretty personable. I was like, 'Yeah, we've got to have this guy back.' "

Soon after Ortiz returned home his manager got a call from the UFC. Ortiz was offered a fight. It would be UFC 18: Road to the Heavyweight Title. Ortiz would face Jerry Bohlander. Ortiz had beaten Bohlander in high school wrestling, but that was years earlier. Since then, Bohlander had joined the Lion's Den and ripped through numerous opponents to become the first UFC lightweight (under two hundred pounds) champion. He lost the title but was back on the winning track.

The UFC offered Ortiz $7,500 to fight. Ortiz jumped at the chance. At the time, it was a large sum of money to him. He thought he could beat Bohlander,

but as the fight drew near doubt crept in. A month before the fight, Ortiz agreed to compete in a "tune-up" fight for a local promotional company called the West Coast No-Holds-Barred Championships. He wanted to test his skills. His opponent was Jeremy Screeton. Many of Ortiz's friends were in the stands, including members of the heavy metal band KoRn, with whom Ortiz had developed a friendship.

The fight with Screeton was over in a flash. The fighters traded punches, locked up, and Ortiz bashed Screeton in the head with knee kicks. Screeton tapped out sixteen seconds into the fight. Ortiz figured he was ready for Bohlander.

UFC 18 was held in New Orleans, Louisiana, on January 8, 1999. Ortiz's match with Bohlander was

A panoramic view of downtown New Orleans

the fourth of seven bouts on the fight card that night. It was scheduled for one fifteen-minute round. Ortiz entered the octagon with shorts in a flame design along with a new nickname: The Huntington Beach Bad Boy. Bohlander was not impressed. He said in interviews that his grandmother could hit harder than Ortiz and that Ortiz had no chance. Bohlander was wrong.

From the start, Ortiz dominated the fight. He landed an overhand right, then grabbed Bohlander's legs for a double leg takedown. He pushed Bohlander's head against the cage and pounded him with fists and elbows. Bohlander escaped. Standing toe to toe, Ortiz rocked Bohlander with several uppercuts. Then he took him to the ground again, wrapped his legs around him in the open guard position, and delivered more blows. Bohlander wriggled free and got to his feet. Ortiz stalked him. He connected with more knees and punches, then took the Lion's Den fighter back to the ground. He pressed Bohlander's head against the cage again. The pounding continued. At the 14:31 mark, referee John McCarthy mercifully stopped the fight.

Bohlander had suffered a fierce beating. Ortiz threw his arms in the air and pranced around the Octagon. He strode to Bohlander's corner where an army of Lion's Den members stood. He pretended his fingers were guns, fired them at the Lion's Den, and blew on the barrels. Then he put on a crude shirt with a curse word. Asterisks replaced two letters to avoid spelling out the word, but everyone knew what it meant. "I wasn't all that crazy about the shirt," matchmaker Silva said. "It was a pretty harsh shirt. I thought it was somewhat funny. I'm sure the Lion's Den didn't find it that funny."

Neither did the media. One publication even called Ortiz "a cartoon character." They didn't know that shortly before the fight an adult film company had offered Ortiz $2,000 to wear the shirt. To make such money in a few minutes' time was something Ortiz couldn't pass up. Besides, it helped stir things up with the Lion's Den, which was Ortiz's intention. He enraged them further when he said after the fight, "I've got to fight all these alley cats and send them all back to their litter box." The Lion's Den sought revenge. Everyone, that is, except Jerry Bohlander. After Ortiz's beat down, Bohlander would never fight in the UFC again.

The History of the Ultimate Fighting Championship

Can a boxer beat a judo expert? Can a wrestler beat a karate black belt? Sports fans often wondered such things. On November 12, 1993, at McNichols Sports Arena in Denver, Colorado, a contest was held to find out.

The idea was hatched by ad man Art Davie and martial arts master Rorion Gracie. They called it War of the Worlds. Semaphore Entertainment Group (SEG) televised the event on pay-per-view. A SEG employee referred to it as the Ultimate Fighting Championship and the name stuck. The event was later renamed UFC 1: The Beginning. The eight-man, single-elimination tournament featured, among other disciplines, two kickboxers, a shootfighter, and a sumo wrestler. The winner was Royce Gracie, a Brazilian Jiu Jitsu black belt and Gracie's younger brother.

The event drew 86,592 TV subscribers, which was considered a success.

UFC 44: Undisputed at Mandalay Bay
Hotel and Casino in Nevada in 2003

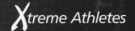

"That show was only supposed to be a one-off," current UFC president Dana White said. "It did so well on pay-per-view they decided to do another, and another. Never in a million years did these guys think they were creating a sport." Four months later, a sixteen-man tournament called UFC 2: No Way Out was held with Gracie winning again.

The early UFC bouts had no weight classes, matching fighters of widely varying sizes. Two separate weight classes (heavyweight over two hundred pounds; lightweight 199 and under) were introduced in 1997. There were only three ways to end a fight—knockout, submission, or throwing in the towel. That is, there were no decisions, and consequently, no judges. One fight at UFC 5: The Return of the Beast was a singles fight, and so was not part of the tournament. That fight, between Royce Gracie and Ken Shamrock, lasted over thirty-six minutes and had to be declared a draw because both fighters were too exhausted to continue to fight. The tournament style was phased out in 1998, with all contests held as singles fights.

The UFC touted its combat sport with the phrase "There are no rules!" and disallowed only biting and eye gouging. The early fights permitted groin strikes, head-butting, and fish-hooking (finger-ripping the cheeks), among other violent techniques.

Government authorities stepped in to legislate the sport, and many states outlawed it. Stricter rules were implemented to ease concerns. The sport experienced moderate success, but SEG was on the verge of bankruptcy, and so advertising was minimal. In 2001, Station Casinos executives Frank and Lorenzo Fertitta bought the UFC for $2 million and created Zuffa, LLC as its parent company (zuffa means "to fight" in Italian). Dana White was named president and given 9 percent ownership. Lorenzo Fertitta was a former member of the Nevada State Athletic Commission, and his connections influenced that state to allow events to be held at ritzy casinos. Zuffa invested heavily in promotions.

Visibility was increased in 2005 with the creation of a reality television show, *The Ultimate Fighter (TUF)*, which aired on Spike TV to much fanfare. A second weekly program, *UFC Unleashed*, followed. UFC's pay-per-view buy rate exploded. In 2006, the promotion generated more than $222,766,000 in pay-per-view revenue, surpassing both boxing and pro wrestling. That same year, Zuffa bought out competitor World Fighting Alliance. Japan-based rival Pride Fighting Championships was acquired one year later. In 2010, the UFC merged with its sister promotion, World Extreme Cagefighting. In 2011, Zuffa purchased rival Strikeforce. Zuffa controlled all relevant promotions now and nearly all the world's top-ranked fighters. The UFC was king of mixed martial arts. ■

Back home, Ortiz celebrated uncontrollably. "I started partying and hitting the clubs," he said. "Everybody was giving me high fives and I was being recognized. I would party nonstop. I was pretty much out of control." One morning, Garcia got a call from Meyrowitz, the UFC owner. "Can Tito fight Guy Mezger in sixteen days?" Meyrowitz asked. Mezger was scheduled to face Vitor Belfort at UFC 19, but Belfort's knee was injured, and he had to pull out of the fight. Garcia called Ortiz, and they had this exchange:

Ortiz: "There's no way I can be ready. I've been partying like crazy. There's no way I can do it."

Garcia: "Tito, you can do it! If anybody can do it, I know you can."

Ortiz: "Let me go run. I'll call you back."

Ortiz ran on the beach for a few miles. He called Garcia back.

Ortiz: "Absolutely there is no way I can be in shape in time for this fight. I'm totally out of shape. It's not going to work."

Garcia: "Tito. Do it! We'll make great things happen!"

(Pause.)

Ortiz: "OK."

Fighters train several months for a major bout. The fact that Ortiz agreed to face Mezger on such short notice and in poor physical condition impressed

Vitor Belfort at the Affliction Banned mixed martial arts event at the Honda Center in Anaheim, California, in July 2008

UFC officials. Announcer Bruce Buffer said, "You've got to be tough and ready to go at any time, and face whoever with no fear, if you're ever going to be a champion. Guy Mezger is one of the best fighters in the UFC. Very tough. Proven. I thought it was a tough task for Tito. But he took the challenge. That was intestinal fortitude. That was a test and he took it."

Ortiz trained furiously in the little time he had. He tried to improve his stamina by lifting weights, running sprints, jogging, skipping rope, and boxing and wrestling with his training partners. Ortiz was obsessed with getting revenge for his loss to Mezger two years earlier. But was he overtraining? Muay Thai expert Ellis grew concerned. "Tito is throwing up twice a day," he told Garcia. UFC 19: Ultimate Young Guns was held March 5, 1999, in Bay St. Louis, Mississippi.

This time, Ortiz's fight was featured as the main event. Ortiz was ready for the occasion. He shot at Mezger and took him down. He controlled Mezger with a half guard and pounded him with elbows and fists. Mezger wrapped his arms around Ortiz's neck and started to squeeze. It was the same move he had used to subdue Ortiz the first time. But Ortiz was wiser now, and he had learned to escape such holds. He pulled his head free. He moved Mezger toward the cage and pounded him again. Mezger escaped to his feet, but Ortiz pulled him right back down for more punishment. Mezger spun onto his stomach. Ortiz jabbed sharp elbows into the back of Mezger's head. Mezger escaped twice more, but both times Ortiz brought him back to the ground. He pounded on Mezger's head and back with hammer fists. Mezger was unable to fight back.

Ortiz hammered away as he looked up at referee McCarthy, wondering if he would ever stop the fight. McCarthy finally did at the 9:55 mark. The crowd roared as Ortiz sprang to his feet and fired his pistol fingers. Then he donned another vulgar shirt that mocked Mezger. Ken Shamrock, the leader of the Lion's Den, climbed to the top of the Octagon railing and screamed obscenities. "Tito! Don't let me catch you wearing that T-shirt!" he yelled. The Lion's Den seethed.

Back near the dressing rooms, men were yelling and tables were getting flipped. Security from all parts of the Casino Magic poured in to keep the two camps separated. For Ortiz, the night was a great success. He had established his image now. He was the Huntington Beach Bad Boy. Everyone would want to see him fight again.

Tito with his team of martial artists, Team Punishment

five
Punishment

O rtiz had positioned himself
perfectly. Mixed martial arts
expert and magazine editor
Clyde Gentry III explained it this way:

> You have to have some
> type of bravado that's
> going to allow the audi-
> ence to buy into the rea-
> son why they're pay-
> ing money to watch you.
> Ortiz had a way of doing
> it. He had the flame shorts.
> He had the shirt. His hair
> was dyed. He was almost
> devilish. That helped him
> with his star appeal. Being
> put over with the crowd

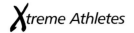

doesn't necessarily mean you have to
be a good guy. It just means you have
to be somebody that people, either way,
want to see.

Now Ortiz needed to keep winning. The problem
was, he lost his next fight.

UFC 22: There Can Be Only One Champion
took place on September 24, 1999, in Lake Charles,
Louisiana. Ortiz was matched against middleweight
champion Frank Shamrock, Ken Shamrock's younger
brother. It was the main event, and Ortiz would cap-
ture the title belt with a victory. He signed a contract
for $25,000 for the fight. When he found out later that
the UFC had cut the sum to $10,000 and that his man-
ager Garcia did not try to stop them, he fired Garcia.
"But the money really wasn't the most important thing
to me," Ortiz said. "I fought for the love of fighting
and for the attention that I never got as a kid."

Shamrock was a veteran who had defended his
title three times already. He knew all the tricks. Under
new UFC rules, title fights were five rounds of five
minutes each, and as Ortiz was about to discover,
twenty-five minutes is a long time to fight.

Ortiz dominated early. He repeatedly took down
Shamrock and landed elbows and fists. He won the
first three rounds this way. In the fourth round Ortiz
was in control again, but he was running out of

Tito Ortiz

energy. His blows were losing their steam.

Late in the round, Shamrock unloaded a flurry of punches that hurt Ortiz. The fighters got to their feet. Ortiz shot in again but could only grab Shamrock's ankle. Shamrock pounded

Frank Shamrock

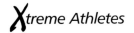

Ortiz on the back of the head. Ortiz was exhausted. He tapped out.

In the octagon afterward, Ortiz was devastated. He put on an autographed Frank Shamrock shirt out of respect. He had trained six months for this fight and just assumed he would be a UFC champion, but instead he learned a valuable lesson. "I was just going to bulldoze over him," Ortiz said. "If I had put a game plan together against Frank I would have won. I should have relaxed in a lot of positions. I took that loss as a win because I learned so much from it. I learned how to pace myself."

After the fight, a boy asked Ortiz if he had a T-shirt for sale with his name on it. Ortiz didn't, but it gave him an idea. At home, his brother Marty praised him for the punishment he gave Shamrock. *Punishment.* Ortiz liked that word. He decided to print the word on T-shirts with TitoOrtiz.com under it. The T-shirts sold. He had dozens of pairs of TitoOrtiz.com shorts made with the flame design he wore in his fights. Fans bought the shorts too. Ortiz created a new clothing line. He called the company Punishment Athletics. Kristin helped him run the operation. Later, they would add jackets, sweat pants, hats, and beanies.

Ortiz wanted a rematch with Frank Shamrock. Shamrock wouldn't give it to him. Instead, he retired from the UFC. The middleweight title was now vacant. Ortiz trained harder than ever. He wanted to improve his fighting skills in every way he could, in case the UFC offered him a shot at the title. He worked out with Chuck Liddell, another budding fighter. Together they sparred and grappled and taught each other moves. Ortiz wanted more. He called Frank Shamrock. They trained together for two weeks. Shamrock taught Ortiz new ways to build endurance and how to keep it during a fight. Sure enough, the UFC called to offer Ortiz another chance at the title. His opponent would be Wanderlei Silva, an aggressive Brazilian striker with a piercing glare and a fight game to back it up. Silva's nickname was "The Axe Murderer."

UFC 25: Ultimate Japan 3 took place April 4, 2000, in Tokyo, Japan. Ortiz controlled Silva from the start. For the first two rounds, he repeatedly pulled the Brazilian to the ground and hit him, though not with his usual force. He did not want to wear himself out. In the third round, Silva rocked Ortiz with a knee kick and then a straight left hand that staggered him. Silva launched a volley of kicks and punches to finish him off. If Ortiz hadn't saved his energy, he might have been knocked out. As it was, he survived the flurry, then shot in and took Silva to the ground. Silva won the round, but nothing more. Ortiz controlled the final two rounds—and then it was over. The announcement came: a unanimous decision by the judges for the *new middleweight champion of the world . . . Tito Ortiz!* Ortiz fired his victory guns.

He put on a shirt that read: "I Just Killed an Axe Murderer." He felt on top of the world. Back home, he slept with his title belt for a month.

Dana White signed on to manage Ortiz. White was new to the business, but he was aggressive, and Ortiz liked that. White had just agreed to manage Chuck Liddell too. White secured a new contract for Ortiz to fight three times at more than $80,000 per event.

Ortiz was a celebrity now. In public, people approached him for autographs and to have their picture taken with him. At nightclubs, they surrounded him and bought him drinks. Ortiz loved the attention; Kristin did not. "Fans tended to look at Tito like he was God and not a real person," she said. "And nobody knew who I was. I was always getting knocked over and pushed out of the way."

Ortiz sensed that he and Kristin were growing apart. He did not want to lose her. So he did the only thing he could think of. He asked her to marry him. They were married in June 2000. "The wedding was amazing," Kristin said. "We wrote and recited our own vows. Tito cried. But then, Tito cries a lot. He's just this big, emotional guy."

The newlyweds left for Bermuda on their honeymoon. The first day there, disaster struck. Ortiz and Kristin were riding through the streets on a rented moped with Ortiz driving and Kristin on the back. At a stop sign, Ortiz looked the wrong way and lurched forward—directly in front of a bus. The impact sent

A beach in Bermuda

Ortiz flying twenty feet through the air and skidding across the pavement. Kristin was pinned under the bus. They were taken by ambulance to the hospital. Ortiz had road rash all over his body. Kristin had suffered broken vertebrae and ribs. They spent three days in the hospital and then flew home. It took Ortiz two months to recover. It took Kristin six.

In the meantime, Ortiz lost his new manager. Casino operators Frank and Lorenzo Fertitta bought the UFC. White and Lorenzo were childhood friends. White was given the position of UFC president, and he appointed attorney James Gallows to be Ortiz's new manager. Ortiz wondered if such an arrangement was in his best interest, but he trusted White. His primary concern was keeping his title belt. Several challengers were lined up to take it.

Ortiz's first defense came at UFC 29: Defense of the Belts on December 16, 2000, in Tokyo. Hometown favorite Yuki Kondo was a dangerous striker who had won twenty-nine times, including a knockout of Frank Shamrock with vicious kicks. Sure enough, just seconds into the fight, Kondo knocked Ortiz to the floor was a fierce knee kick. But Ortiz popped up and came directly at Kondo. He grabbed Kondo's legs and drove him into the ground. He slammed him with fists and elbows and finished him off with a high half nelson. The official result was a submission by neck crank at 1:51 of the first round. Many in the crowd booed afterward as Ortiz pretended to dig a grave to bury Kondo.

Two months later, Ortiz was back in the Octagon. UFC 30: Battle on the Boardwalk took place February 23, 2001, in Atlantic City, New Jersey. The new UFC owners were investing heavily in the sport. Ortiz was flown across the country in a Lear jet. Ortiz had become the face of the sport now. Posters and logos advertising the event showed him standing with his arms on his hips wearing his championship belt.

The contest was held at the Trump Taj Mahal. Ortiz's opponent was Evan Tanner, who was undefeated in UFC events and a future middleweight champion. At the bell, Ortiz threw a leg kick. Tanner grabbed at him. Ortiz kneed Tanner in the stomach and punched him in the face. Then he wrapped his arms around Tanner and squeezed him in a body lock. He lifted Tanner and slammed him to the ground. Tanner was knocked out on impact. The fight was over in twenty seconds.

Inevitably, some wondered if Ortiz took performance enhancing drugs. An interviewer asked him about steroids. "Anybody who takes steroids to make them bigger?" Ortiz said. "They are weak-minded, and they probably have a weak heart too."

Among Ortiz's secrets was his training ground. He worked out at Big Bear Lake above Los Angeles at 7,000 feet elevation. Such altitude training, with its relative lack of oxygen, increases an athlete's endurance. "Every day I box, I eat, I wrestle, I eat, I go run and lift, then I go to bed," Ortiz said. "That's my job. I train."

Ortiz's next defense came on June 29, 2001, at UFC 32: Showdown in the Meadowlands in East

Rutherford, New Jersey. The venue was Continental Airlines Arena—the largest stage yet for a UFC event. The middleweight division had been renamed "light heavyweight." To Ortiz, it didn't matter—it was still a championship fight.

Ortiz's opponent this time was Elvis Sinosic, an

Australian fighter known as "The King of Rock N Rumble." Sinosic missed a kick to start the fight and all was lost. Ortiz bull-rushed him and unloaded several overhand bombs. He shoved Sinosic against the cage and threw more fists and elbows. Then he dropped to his back in the guard position and opened up a gruesome cut on Sinosic's forehead. He continued to rain punches into Sinosic until referee John McCarthy stopped the fight at 3:22 of the first round. Ortiz fired off his trademark pistols and was surrounded by his ever-growing posse,

Downtown Las Vegas, home of the UFC

including singer Fred Durst of the rock band Limp Bizkit and former National Basketball Association star Dennis Rodman.

Three months later, Ortiz was back in the Octagon for UFC 33: Victory in Vegas. The event was held September 28, 2001, at the Mandalay Bay Events Center on the Las Vegas strip. It was the first UFC fight sanctioned by the Nevada State Athletic Commission, marking a significant advancement of the sport. The poster for the event showed Ortiz matched against Vitor Belfort of Brazil, but an arm injury to Belfort just a week beforehand paved the way for a Russian Olympic wrestler named Vladimir Matyushenko.

Ortiz was in for a prolonged battle this time. He entered the Octagon carrying the American flag amid chants of "U-S-A! U-S-A!" from the overflow crowd. The fight went the full five rounds. Ortiz out-wrestled

and out-punched the Russian, and he won every round on the judges' scorecards for a unanimous decision.

Back home, Kristin was pregnant. Ortiz was both thrilled and scared to be a father. He didn't want his child to grow up as he had, living in a garage or rummaging through garbage cans for food. He wanted to be sure his child had plenty of everything. The UFC's success was soaring, and Ortiz knew he was a big reason why. He asked Gallows to negotiate a contract for more money, but Gallows seemed incapable of influencing Dana White. So Ortiz went directly to White. He was told to be patient.

On June 1, 2002, Ortiz's son Jacob was born. Ortiz was angry with his own mother and father for the way he was raised, but he had made peace with his mother a year earlier, and now he reached out to his father. Samuel met his grandson at Ortiz's house one day, but the reconnection ended there.

MGM Grand Hotel in Las Vegas

six

The Reign Ends

O rtiz's popularity had reached new heights. He was featured in a video game. His likeness was made into an action figure. He acted in the movie *Cradle 2 the Grave* in which he played a cage fighter. He was considered by many to be the best fighter at any level in the UFC, a reputation he cemented on November 22, 2002, at UFC 40: Vendetta.

More than 13,000 fans filled the MGM Grand Arena in Las Vegas to see Ortiz face legendary former champion Ken Shamrock, the leader of the Lion's Den. The feud between Ortiz and the Lion's Den had been brewing for years, and the largest audience ever for a UFC event tuned in to see what would happen. More than 150,000 pay-per-view television buys

netted the UFC nearly $6 million. Viewers saw total domination by Ortiz.

Moments after the opening bell, he pressed Shamrock against the cage where he buried knees and right hands into Shamrock's body. Then he pulled Shamrock to the ground and pounded him with fists and elbows for four straight minutes. Somehow Shamrock didn't lose consciousness. In Round 2, Shamrock came out swinging wildly, and Ortiz easily took him down to the ground again. He pounded elbows into Shamrock's head for several minutes, and by now, Shamrock's face was swollen and bloody. Shamrock was able to scramble to his feet and land one feeble left hand. Round 3 was another ruthless ground-and-pound clinic for Ortiz. Shamrock staggered to his corner and could barely move. At the bell for Round 4, Shamrock stayed on his stool. He was finished. On a technical knockout, it was over. The crowd roared as Ortiz fired his pistols and donned his victory shirt.

For the first time, the UFC was receiving mainstream media attention. ESPN and other television sports networks showed highlights. Major metropolitan newspapers printed stories. Ortiz knew he was a big reason why. He approached Dana White for more

Tito, right, lands a right hit to Ken Shamrock during the Ultimate Fighting Championship light heavyweight title fight at the MGM Grand Hotel and Casino in Las Vegas in November 2002.

money for his next fight. "If it wasn't for me," White told Ortiz, "you'd be nothing."

For the most part, White was right. While Ortiz was the one training hard and destroying opponents in the Octagon, White was responsible for arranging and promoting the events. If Ortiz somehow disappeared another fighter would simply take his place. But if the UFC ceased operations, where would Ortiz go? Competing promotions weren't nearly as popular.

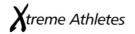

Ortiz needed the UFC more than the UFC needed Ortiz. As it was, Ortiz's frustration with White created a rift that would deepen over time.

For Ortiz's next title defense the UFC wanted him to fight Chuck Liddell. Liddell had worked his way up to top-contender status. It seemed to be the perfect matchup. But Ortiz and Liddell were friends. They had trained together at Big Bear Lake. Ortiz didn't like the idea of fighting his friend. More than that, he was unhappy with the UFC's offer to him of $160,000 for the fight. Ortiz knew the company would make several million dollars from TV revenue and gate receipts. He wanted a bigger share of it. The UFC didn't budge on its offer. So Ortiz didn't fight. The UFC scrambled to put together UFC 43: Meltdown. Ortiz's replacement was former UFC heavyweight champion Randy Couture.

The fight between Liddell and Couture was for the "interim" light heavyweight title. It meant the title would be held temporarily by the winner until it could be determined if Ortiz was coming back. Ortiz was furious. He felt the UFC had betrayed him. Was Ortiz being greedy? UFC fans argued about it. Meanwhile, Couture defeated Liddell to claim the interim title. While fight fans enjoyed that battle, Ortiz's absence was glaring. As one online publication simply wrote: "Tito Ortiz, where are you?"

The UFC offered Ortiz one more chance. For the same money, he could fight Couture. If he did not accept, he would forfeit his title. Still seething, Ortiz agreed. He figured he would exact revenge on White and the UFC by crushing Couture.

Ortiz spent three months at Big Bear, but midway through his training he was beset by stabbing back pain. Doctors diagnosed a bulging disc for which Ortiz was given pills to ease the suffering. He pressed on with his training and was able to run, lift weights, and practice Jiu-Jitsu, but his aggravated back hindered his wrestling training. Couture's strength was wrestling, and the setback did not bode well for Ortiz.

UFC 44: Undisputed was held on September 26, 2003, at the Mandalay Bay in Las Vegas. Ortiz was overpowered from the start. Couture body slammed him to the ground and pounded on him with hard elbows. Ortiz gained top control for a moment, but Couture muscled him into a submissive position and beat on him more to win the first round. It got worse for Ortiz. Couture bullied him through the middle rounds to take complete control. Ortiz needed a knockout. In Round 5, he landed a big right hand. Couture didn't blink. Ortiz was taken down once more and finished off with hammer fists. He lost a unanimous decision. With tears in his eyes, Ortiz put the light heavyweight title belt around Couture's waist. It was his first loss in more than four years, and the feeling overwhelmed him. "It was like a loved one dying," he said. "It just hurt so much."

UFC Basics

UFC matches are held in an eight-sided cage called an Octagon. The Octagon is thirty-two feet wide. The fence is made of black vinyl similar in form to a playground fence and is five-and-one-half feet high. Two gates are on opposite sides of the fence. During the match, only the two fighters and the referee are allowed inside the Octagon. Between rounds, assistants (cornermen) are permitted inside to provide treatment and advice.

Rounds are five minutes each. A contest for a championship belt is five rounds. All other matches are three rounds. There is a one-minute rest between rounds. Fighters are grouped into classes based on weight. The seven weight divisions are bantamweight (126 to 135 pounds), featherweight (136-145), lightweight (146-155), welterweight (156-170), middleweight (171-185), light heavyweight (186-205), and heavyweight (206-265). Fighters must wear approved shorts and open-fingered gloves with padding at least one-inch thick around the knuckles. Nothing else can be worn.

Two cage fighters grapple in the Octagon.

Fights are decided in four ways:

Submission—the fighter declares quitting by tapping on the mat or his opponent. This is commonly known as tapping out.

Knockout (KO)— the fighter loses consciousness.

Technical Knockout (TKO)—the fighter is declared finished by the referee (in the referee's judgment the fighter no longer has the ability to defend himself), the ringside doctor (due to excessive bleeding or serious injury), or the fighter's own cornermen.

Judges' Decision—on a fight that goes the distance, three judges score the fight and render their decision. If all three judges agree on the winner, it is a unanimous decision. If two judges agree on the winner, while the other judge declares it a tie, it is a majority decision. If two judges agree on the winner, while the other judge scores a win for the loser, it is a split decision. If the scoring comes out equal, it is a draw (tie).

State athletic commissions and the UFC work together to enforce a long list of fouls. Among the most flagrant are head-butting, eye-gouging, hair-pulling, biting, groin attacks, fish-hooking, throat strikes, clawing, pinching, and kicking or kneeing the head of a grounded opponent. ■

Ortiz sank into a depression. Kristin could not cheer him up. "I was hard on myself for two solid months," he said. "I cried all the time." The UFC offered little sympathy. When a reporter asked White how Ortiz fit in the UFC's plans, White replied, "You know I hate Tito. Why are you asking about him?" But White was a businessman, and he understood Ortiz's value to his company. The fact was, fans still wanted to see Ortiz fight.

The obvious matchup was arranged, and the event's title said it all—UFC 47: It's On. Ortiz would face "The Iceman" Chuck Liddell. Ortiz was paid $125,000 for the fight. Liddell was paid $50,000. The winner would receive a bonus of $50,000.

Ortiz was eager to redeem himself. There were several forces working against him. His popularity prompted an offer from another movie company that he couldn't refuse, and so he interrupted his training to act in the film *The Crow: Wicked Prayer*. His relationship with Kristin was on the verge of collapse, largely due to Ortiz's infidelity and his life of fame that hardly included her. For this, he sought therapy, and he said the sessions left him soft and vulnerable— not the right frame of mind to be leading into a fight. Finally, the bout was against his friend Liddell. And as much he tried, Ortiz could not muster the requisite anger he needed to feel toward his opponent in order to want to annihilate him.

Tito counters Chuck Liddell before being knocked out in the second round at the UFC fight at Mandalay Bay in 2004.

The contest took place April 2, 2004, at the Mandalay Bay, with celebrities such as actors Juliette Lewis and George Clooney ringing the first few rows around the Octagon. Ortiz entered the arena carrying a large flag representing America on one side and Mexico on the other to honor his mixed-race heritage. With the crowd on its feet throughout, and at one point chanting "Ti-to! Ti-to!" the first round was more like a boxing match with the fighters exchanging a few punches. Ortiz attempted takedowns twice, but Liddell sprawled free from both. Liddell opened the second round with an accidental poke of his thumb into Ortiz's eye. Ortiz's vision was blurred. Liddell attacked with a lethal combination that pushed Ortiz to the cage. A barrage of punches pummeled Ortiz. He dropped. Referee John McCarthy covered him and ended it. Ortiz lost. He hugged Liddell and praised him afterward as the better fighter. Ortiz's reign of supremacy was suddenly over. So was his marriage with Kristin. Their lifestyles were just too different, and they agreed to part as friends.

Tito enters the arena during UFC 73: Stacked at the
ARCO Arena in Sacramento, California, in July 2007.

seven

Back at Full Force

If Ortiz was reeling from his losses, he never showed it. He was back in the Octagon for UFC 50: The War of '04, where he controlled Patrick Cote for a unanimous decision. At UFC 51: Super Saturday, he defeated former champion Vitor Belfort despite suffering a broken nose. His popularity was sky high. But negotiations for a new contract collapsed. Ortiz wanted more than the UFC was willing to give. Both sides dug in their heels. The impasse grew so bitter that Ortiz and his Team Punishment company were removed from the UFC's Web site. Ortiz responded by removing the

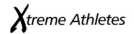

UFC from his radar. The standoff lasted more than a year.

Ortiz was wooed by competing promotions like Pride Fighting Championships and the World Fighting Alliance. He nearly signed a six-fight deal with Pride before considering it a lateral move. Instead, he appeared as a guest referee for Total Nonstop Action Wrestling just to keep his name in the public. He didn't want people to forget about him.

That wasn't about to happen.

A groundswell of support to see Ortiz return to the UFC was enough to sway White and the Fertitta brothers to negotiate with him again. Ortiz agreed to a three-fight contract—and the starring role on a TV show. *The Ultimate Fighter* was a reality series on Spike TV that showed two camps of fighters who train and compete. Ortiz was the coach for one team; Ken Shamrock was coach for the other. The toxic history between the two fighters provided for a natural rivalry. Ortiz clearly got the best of Shamrock as his team won nine of the twelve fights. After the thirteen episodes concluded, Ortiz and Shamrock fought in a UFC main event.

First, while the show was airing, Ortiz faced emerging star Forrest Griffin at UFC 59: Reality Check. The event was held April 15, 2006, in Anaheim, California. A sold-out crowd at Arrowhead Pond watched Ortiz win a split decision. His T-shirt afterward said: "With Great Sacrifice Comes Great Rewards."

Next up was Shamrock. UFC 61: Bitter Rivals occurred July 8, 2006, at the Mandalay Bay and set a UFC record for pay-per-view buys at 775,000. Ortiz earned $210,000 for the fight. He threw Shamrock to the ground and buried elbows into his head until referee Herb Dean stopped the fight just 1:18 into the first round. Ortiz put on a shirt that said: "If You Fight Tito Ortiz You Lose!" Shamrock complained that the fight had been stopped too soon. A rematch was held October 10, 2006, in Hollywood, Florida, and was billed as Ortiz vs. Shamrock 3: The Final Chapter. It was shown live on Spike TV with a record 5.7 million viewers tuned in. Ortiz destroyed Shamrock again, knocking him out with punches 2:23 into the first round. This time, his T-shirt read: "Punishing Him Into Retirement." Ortiz had rebuilt his reputation as a dangerous fighter and contentious showman.

Ortiz shared custody of his son Jacob, and he and Kristin remained good friends. In the summer of 2006, Ortiz started a new relationship with Jenna Marie Massoli. Jenna had starred in the adult film industry under the name Jenna Jameson. They corresponded on Myspace and by e-mail before meeting in person at a UFC promotion in Las Vegas. A few days later, Ortiz asked her on a date to the county fair. They fell in love, and a year later Ortiz said, "She's not with

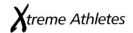

me for my money. The fact is she has more money than I do. We're kind of like a celebrity power couple and we empower each other." Two years after that, Ortiz and Jenna had twin boys—Jesse and Journey.

In the meantime, Ortiz's success in the Octagon went sideways. In a much-hyped rematch with Chuck Liddell at UFC 66: Ortiz vs. Liddell 2, on December 30, 2006, at the Mandalay Bay, Ortiz lost on a technical knockout with one minute left in the fight. The show was a commercial success, how-

Mandalay Bay Resort and Casino in Las Vegas

ever, eclipsing the 1-million mark for pay-per-view purchases for the first time. Ortiz was paid $210,000 for the fight, plus a small percentage of the pay-per-view profit, and afterward he wore a shirt that read: "Thanks U.S. Troops For Fighting For Our Country."

Chuck Liddell, top, pounds Tito in the third round of the
Ultimate Fighting Championship in Las Vegas in December 2006.

On July 7, 2007, at UFC 73: Stacked, he fought undefeated Rashad Evans to a draw and wore a shirt that said: "Bad Boy For Life." On May 24, 2008, at UFC 84: Ill Will, he lost a unanimous decision to Lyoto Machida. On November 11, 2009, at UFC 106: Ortiz vs. Griffin 2, he suffered a heartbreaking split decision loss to Forrest Griffin. On October 23, 2010, at UFC 121: Lesnar vs. Velasquez, he lost a unanimous decision to Matt "The Hammer" Hamill, a deaf fighter whom Ortiz had trained in *The Ultimate Fighter.*

The string of losses frustrated Ortiz. They could be attributed, at least in part, to his chronic back problems that limited his training and required two surgeries. But by now he was earning nearly 1 million dollars per fight. His popularity seemed to transcend winning. He wanted to win, of course, and he took extra measures to commit more time to training, even spending $2.1 million to buy boxer Oscar de la Hoya's house at Big Bear Lake so he could live there and train.

But much of his focus went beyond the Octagon, especially toward acting. He appeared in three movies—the police drama *Venice Underground*, the romantic comedy *Dog Problem*, and the war film *Valley of the Wolves,* in which he played a U.S. military commander. He appeared on an episode of the television series *Numb3rs* and starred in Donald

Trump's *Celebrity Apprentice*. Ortiz was particularly beloved by service troops. The U.S. Department of Defense invited him to Washington, D.C., to meet with wounded soldiers at Bethesda Hospital and Walter Reed Army Hospital, and to Iraq to visit with combat troops.

In March 2011, Ortiz's Punishment Training Center in Huntington Beach opened to the public. He works with aspiring fighters at the center, even as he continues to train for upcoming UFC events. Whether or not Ortiz returns to the sport's pinnacle, his legacy is assured. He was the poster boy for the UFC's rise to prominence and will be remembered as perhaps the most colorful personality in its history. His behavior as a mixed martial artist was sometimes shocking, and even Ortiz's Web site states that he is a "controversial and highly-criticized fighter." But such antics were purposeful and successful in generating the fame he sought. In the bigger picture, the lesson Ortiz's life teaches is explained by Ortiz this way: "It is possible for somebody to start out living a life as a total zero and end up living a life that most people dream about. When you have a dream and you set your goals, you can achieve anything."

Lyoto Machida, right, exchanges blows with Tito during their UFC light heavyweight match at the MGM Grand Garden Arena in Las Vegas in May 2008.

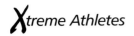

Timeline

1975	Born January 23 in Huntington Beach, California.
1987	Parents, Joyce and Samuel Ortiz, separate.
1989	Joins Huntington Beach High School wrestling team.
1991	Begins working with Coach Paul Herrera.
1993	Amasses a wrestling record of 56-3 and wins league and county title.
1996-1997	Wins back-to-back junior college state titles; wins first UFC fight.
1999	Creates Huntington Beach Bad Boy image.
2000	Defeats Wanderlei Silva to win UFC middleweight title; defends title in Japan; creates Punishment Athletics.
2001-2002	Defends middleweight (later called light heavyweight) title four times to become UFC's most dominant fighter.
2004-2006	Avenges losses with five straight wins; appears in reality TV series and movies.
2007-2011	Becomes perhaps most popular fighter in UFC; appears in several movies; opens Tito's Punishment Training Center in Huntington Beach.

Sources

Chapter One: A Rough Start

p. 11,   "Is that all . . ." Tito Ortiz and Marc Shapiro, *Tito Ortiz: This is Gonna Hurt* (New York: Simon & Schuster, Inc., 2008), 109.

p. 13,   "I was too young . . ." Ibid., 7.

p. 18,   "Dad, look what . . ." Ibid., 18.

p. 20,   "I knew the stuff . . ." Ibid., 33.

p. 21,   "That's it . . ."Ibid., 35.

Chapter Two: Getting a Grip

p. 25, "   Let's get those . . ." Ortiz and Shapiro, *Tito Ortiz: This is Gonna Hurt*, 41.

p. 26,   "Where's the . . ." Ibid., 43.

Chapter Three: Seizing Opportunity

p. 43,   "I'm here . . ." Ortiz and Shapiro, *Tito Ortiz: This is Gonna Hurt*, 70.

p. 44,   "a short, brutal fight . . ." Matt McEwen, The History of the UFC: UFC XIII – Ultimate Force," 411mania.com, http://www.411mania.com/MMA/video_reviews/57126 (July 16, 2007).

p. 44,   "I was pumped . . ." Ortiz and Shapiro, *Tito Ortiz: This is Gonna Hurt*, 70.

pp. 45-46, "I got thrown . . ." Pooch, "UFC Middleweight Champion Tito Ortiz Interview Part 1," *Submission Fighting UK*, October 2, 2001, http://sfuk.tripod.com/interviews_01/tito_interview1.html.

p. 47,   "Ortiz got a . . ." *Shamrock vs. Ortiz: The Untold Truth Behind UFC's Legendary Feud!*, directed by Sal Garcia (Action Guy Films, 2006), DVD.

Chapter Four: The Huntington Beach Bad Boy

p. 51,   "I have a . . ." Garcia, *Shamrock vs. Ortiz: The Untold Truth Behind UFC's Legendary Feud!*

p. 52,   "I'd like to . . ." Ibid.

p. 52,   "Sure. Yes . . ." Ibid.

p. 52,   "Bas was my . . ." Pooch, "UFC Middleweight Champion Tito Ortiz Interview Part 2."

p. 52,   "We needed to . . ." Garcia, *Shamrock vs. Ortiz: The Untold Truth Behind UFC's Legendary Feud!*

p. 53,   "He's a hard . . ." Ibid.

p. 57,   "I wasn't all . . ." Ibid.

p. 57,   "a cartoon character," Jonathan Snowden and Kendall Shields, *The MMA Encyclopedia* (Toronto, Canada: ECW Press, 2010), 318.

p. 57,   "I've got to fight . . ." Garcia, *Shamrock vs. Ortiz: The Untold Truth Behind UFC's Legendary Feud!*

p. 60,   "That show was . . ." Jonathan Strickland, "How the Ultimate Fighting Championship Works," *How Stuff Works*, http://entertainment.howstuffworks.com/ufc4.htm.

p. 62,   "I started partying . . ." Ortiz and Shapiro, *Tito Ortiz: This is Gonna Hurt*, 87-88.

p. 62,   "There's no way . . ." Garcia, *Shamrock vs. Ortiz: The Untold Truth Behind UFC's Legendary Feud!*

p. 64,   "You've got to . . ." Ibid.

p. 64,   "Tito is throwing . . ." Ibid.

p. 65,   "Tito! Don't let . . ." Snowden and Shields, *The MMA Encyclopedia*, 319.

Chapter Five: Punishment

pp. 67-68, "You have to . . ." Garcia, *Shamrock vs. Ortiz: The Untold Truth Behind UFC's Legendary Feud!*

p. 68,   "But the money . . ." Ortiz and Shapiro, *Tito Ortiz: This is Gonna Hurt*, 91-92.

p. 70,   "I was just . . ." Pooch, "UFC Middleweight Champion Tito Ortiz Interview Part 2."

p. 72,   "Fans tended to . . ." Ortiz and Shapiro, *Tito Ortiz: This is Gonna Hurt*, 101.

p. 72,   "The wedding was . . ." Ibid., 104.

p. 75,   "Anybody who takes . . ." Pooch, "UFC Middleweight Champion Tito Ortiz Interview Part 2."

p. 76,   "Every day I . . ." Garcia, *Shamrock vs. Ortiz: The Untold Truth Behind UFC's Legendary Feud!*

Chapter Six: The Reign Ends

p. 83,　"If it wasn't . . ." Ortiz and Shapiro, *Tito Ortiz: This is Gonna Hurt*, 126.

p. 84,　"Tito Ortiz, where . . ." Loretta Hunt, "UFC 43—A Monster Meltdown: Couture Becomes 3-Time Champion," *No Holds Barred News*, http://www.fcfighter.com/news0306.htm (June 7, 2003).

p. 85,　"It was like . . ." Ortiz and Shapiro, *Tito Ortiz: This is Gonna Hurt*, 132-133.

p. 89,　"I was hard . . ." Ibid., 133.

p. 89,　"You know I . . ." Snowden and Shields, *The MMA Encyclopedia*, 318.

Chapter Seven: Back at Full Force

pp. 95-96,　"She's not with . . ." Ortiz and Shapiro, *Tito Ortiz: This is Gonna Hurt*, 162.

p. 99,　"controversial and highly . . ." "Tito Ortiz—The Huntington Beach Bad Boy," 2011, http://www.titoortiz.com/about-tito-ortiz.

p. 99,　"It is possible . . ." Ortiz and Shapiro, *Tito Ortiz: This is Gonna Hurt*, 202.

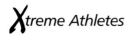

Bibliography

Garcia, Sal. *Shamrock vs. Ortiz: The Untold Truth Behind UFC's Legendary Feud!* DVD, Action Guy Films, 2006.

Hunt, Loretta. "UFC 43—A Monster Meltdown: Couture Becomes 3-Time Champion." *No Holds Barred News*, June 7, 2003. http://www.fcfighter.com/news0306.htm.

McEwen, Matt. "The History of the UFC: UFC XIII—Ultimate Force." 411mania.com, July 16, 2007. http://www.411mania.com/MMA/video_reviews/57126.

Ortiz, Tito, and Marc Shapiro. *Tito Ortiz: This is Gonna Hurt.* New York: Simon & Schuster, 2008.

Pooch. "UFC Middleweight Champion Tito Ortiz Interview Part 1," *Submission Fighting UK*. October 2, 2001. http://sfuk.tripod.com/interviews_01/tito_interview1.html.

Rolling, Leland. "The UFC's Ambitious Global Expansion Plans Could Reap Huge Benefits and Revenues." Bloodyelbow.com, http://www.bloodyelbow.com/2010/6/3/1499271/the-ufcs-ambitious-global.

Sloan, Mike. "Monday Morning Reverie: True Champions." Sherdog.com., July 9, 2007. http://www.sherdog.com/news/articles/Monday-Morning-Reverie-True-Champions-8207.

Snowden, Jonathan, and Kendall Shields. *The MMA Encyclopedia.* Toronto, Canada: ECW Press, 2010.

Strickland, Jonathan. "How the Ultimate Fighting Championship Works." *How Stuff Works.* http://entertainment.howstuffworks.com/ufc4.htm.

Web sites

http://www.titoortiz.com
Tito Ortiz's official site. It includes his biography, photos, videos, recent news about him, and information about his Punishment clothing line, including an online store.

http://www.ufc.com
The Ultimate Fighting Championship official site. It includes upcoming events, results of all UFC fights, overviews of fighters, information on training camps, and the latest news in the UFC.

http://mixedmartialarts.com
This Web site provides information such as event results and statistics, fight videos, and extensive training videos focusing techniques and conditioning.

Index

Photo Credits

All images used in this book not in the public domain are credited in the listing that follows:

Cover: AP Photo/Tammie Arroyo
7: Ross Gilmore / Alamy
8-9: AP Photo/Eric Jamison
10-11: Evan Hurd/Corbis
12-13: Courtesy of DHN
16-17: Used under license from iStockphoto.com
21: Used under license from iStockphoto.com
22: ROGER WILLIAMS/UPI /Landov
26-27: Courtesy of Dreier Carr
31: Used under license from iStockphoto.com
34: AP photo/Marlene Karas
36-37: Used under license from iStockphoto.com
38-39: Courtesy of Don Ramey Logan
42-43: Courtesy of Matthew Tosh
44-45: The structural engineer and amatuer boxer known as east718
47: Courtesy of Lee Brimelow
48: AP Photo/Marlene Karas
50: NCAA Photos via AP Images
54-55: Courtesy of M. Lamar Griffin Sr.
58-59: Barry Bland / Alamy
63: JOHN PYLE/CSM /Landov
66-67: Evan Hurd/Sygma/Corbis
69: Casey Rodgers / AP Images for Xbox 360
72-73: Courtesy of JGHowes
78-79: Courtesy of Chensiyuan
80-81: Songquan Deng / Alamy
82-83: AP Photo/Laura Rauch
86-87: Ross Gilmore / Alamy
90-91: ROGER WILLIAMS/UPI /Landov
92-93: FRANCIS SPECKER/Landov
96-97: Courtesy of Ed Bierman
97: AP Photo/Marlene Karas
100-101: AP Photo/Eric Jamison

Book cover and interior design by Derrick Carroll Creative.